CW00693489

3D
MANDALAS

3D
MANDALAS

WATKINS PUBLISHING
LONDON

3D Mandalas

First published in the UK and USA in 2012 by
Watkins Publishing, an imprint of Duncan Baird Publishers Ltd
Sixth Floor, Castle House
75–76 Wells Street
London W1T 3QH

Conceived, created and designed by Duncan Baird Publishers

Copyright © Duncan Baird Publishers 2012
Text copyright © Duncan Baird Publishers 2012
Artwork copyright © Duncan Baird Publishers 2012
Photograph on page 7 copyright © British Museum, London

All rights reserved. No part of this book may be reproduced in any form or
by any electronic or mechanical means, including information storage and
retrieval systems, without permission in writing from the publisher, except
by a reviewer who may quote brief passages in a review.

Managing Editor: Sandra Rigby
Senior Editor: Fiona Robertson
Designer: Allan Sommerville
Production: Uzma Taj

Text: Jane McIntosh
Consultant: Lisa Tenzin-Dolma
Commissioned artwork: Anne Sharp (pages 15, 19, 35, 39, 51 and 59),
Rowena Dugdale (pages 31, 47 and 55) and Sally Taylor at Artistspartners
(pages 23, 27 and 43)

British Library Cataloguing-in-Publication Data:
A CIP record for this book is available from the British Library

Library of Congress Cataloging-in-Publication Data available

ISBN: 978-1-78028-387-6

10 9 8 7 6 5 4 3 2 1

Typeset in Quadraat
Colour reproduction by XY Digital
Printed in China by Imago

Notes:
Abbreviations used throughout this book:
CE Common Era (the equivalent of AD)
BCE Before the Common Era (the equivalent of BC)

Distributed in the USA and Canada by
Sterling Publishing Co., Inc.
387 Park Avenue South
New York, NY 10016-8810

For information about custom editions, special sales, premium and
corporate purchases, please contact Sterling Special Sales Department
at 800-805-5489 or specialsales@sterlingpub.com.

Duncan Baird Publishers, or any other persons who have been involved in
working on this publication, cannot accept responsibility for any injuries
or damage incurred as a result of following the information, exercises and
techniques contained in this book or from using the accompanying CD.

CONTENTS

INTRODUCTION

A mandala is a symbolic picture used as a tool for meditation in Buddhism, Hinduism and Jainism. It is both a source and a reflection of spiritual energy, and its origins probably date back to the earliest cave paintings.

Mandalas are especially associated with the tantric Buddhism of Tibet, where their highly complex design and often esoteric imagery depict the divine architecture of the cosmos. In Tibetan Buddhism, liturgical texts known as *tantras* provide instructions on how the mandalas should be drawn and visualized, and also indicate which mantras (sacred sounds or phrases) should be recited when mandalas are used in religious rituals.

The natural world with its cycles of birth, life and death provides potent symbols, and natural themes are commonly depicted alongside deities in both religious and non-traditional mandalas. Nature as the creative life force has a "sacred geometry" of universal patterns, rhythms and symmetry and can therefore be seen as the ultimate mandala. Meditating on natural beauty can bring us much spiritual nourishment.

Contemporary mandalas are simpler and more accessible than traditional ones. The mandalas created for this book use symbolism common to many different cultures, as well as images inspired by nature, with a view to helping anyone experiencing the distractions and stresses of modern living to become more focused and tranquil.

Mandala design

The main shape of both traditional and non-traditional mandalas is a disc. The meaning of the Sanskrit word *mandala* is "circle". This shape,

RIGHT: *A traditional Tibetan mandala with Vasudhara, goddess of abundance, at its centre.*

6

with no beginning or end, symbolizes perfection and completion, and its central point represents the spiritual self. The mandala encloses a sacred space within its circumference where tranquillity and peace may be found.

Although the circle is always the primary form of a mandala, other geometric shapes are common, located either within the circle or around the borders. These shapes also have significance: an upward-pointing triangle, for example, represents man's ascent to the Divine, whereas pointing downward it represents the Divine reaching to man; an inverted semi-circle may represent the dome of the heavens; and a square sometimes represents the four cardinal directions of the earthly plane, as well as security and balance.

Colours, too, may convey symbolic meaning, and are often associated with the seasons, and warmth or coolness. Although there are many specific cultural connotations, white is generally considered to be the symbol of purity, yellow is associated with light and the divine principle, red is for energy and life force, green represents nature, blue is for serenity and infinity, and purple often signifies mysticism and spiritual attainment. Buddhist mandalas traditionally use four basic colours – white, yellow, red and green – to represent the four directions (east, south, west and north); colours are also associated with the four elements – blue or black for air, white for water, red for fire and yellow for earth.

Benefits of meditation

Meditation originated in Eastern religion, but you do not need to be religious to practise it. In fact, meditation has been embraced in the West as much for the many psychological and health benefits it offers as for the spiritual dimension. Aside from helping us to explore our unconscious minds and look at ourselves (and others) with honesty and kind understanding, there are other well-documented benefits of meditation: it is a wonderful way of taking time out to calm the mind and relax the body amid the "chatter" and stress of everyday life; it may help in lowering blood pressure, relieving pain and promoting restful sleep (which in turn improves our physical appearance); and it trains the mind to concentrate and focus, thereby boosting mental power.

Through mindful awareness of our surroundings and experience, and by tuning in to the present moment, we are able to find peace and nourish our spiritual and emotional well-being. Contemplating the beauty of nature and reflecting on the inter-connectedness of all things can be of great comfort as it enables us to realize that we are part of a greater whole. Advanced practitioners of meditation describe finding "enlightenment" – a blissful spiritual experience of love and oneness with the ultimate unity from which the cosmos arises.

Using mandalas for meditation

Meditation is a means of quietening the mind to gain insights and the mandala acts as a tool of reflection by which we may recognize our true self. Visual imagery creates particularly powerful associations in the mind, and by meditating on a mandala we are able to shift our inner focus away from the distractions of this world to an internal world of self-awareness, self-acceptance, wisdom and compassion. Focusing attention so that we *really* see what is in front of our eyes is something we rarely do. As the mandala is absorbed into our mind, our mental state and feelings change in a way that makes this level of perception possible. By meditating on the mandala to the point of internalizing every detail, it may be possible to visualize the image at will, whenever it is needed.

At first it may be difficult to focus – external stimuli and peripheral thoughts and worries can distract us. Remember that it is normal for such intrusions to occur when you are meditating. Whenever this happens, simply acknowledge the thoughts but dismiss them to the back of your mind while you refocus and turn your attention to where you choose to be. With practice you will more able to keep external thoughts at a distance, as a sort of "background music".

Loving kindness

Buddhism teaches all-embracing love, kindness and compassion.
In order to enact this, practitioners seek to follow the noble path of
non-violence, to become selfless and part of the One. Mandalas that
are created through the intuitive wisdom of the unconscious mind are
symbolic representations of that underlying unity. Their harmony and
balance express at an unspoken, unconscious level how everything and
everyone is connected. If we allow them to communicate with us, they
can reveal the unifying, all-sustaining love that many spiritual traditions
hold is the source of all creation. Those who experience this ultimate
reality through meditation find that their lives are changed for ever.

One of Buddhism's oldest forms of meditation is the loving-kindness
meditation, which encourages feelings of love toward ourselves and
others, so that we become more patient, accepting and compassionate.
According to Buddhist thought, the path to true happiness lies in
becoming less self-centred. We do this by being able to empathize with
others, by seeing their suffering and helping them. In this book you will

find a mandala meditation to help you to be kind and forgiving to both yourself and to other people (see pages 30–33).

How to use this book

For each of the 12 mandalas in this book you are invited to follow a guided meditation (newcomers to mandala meditation may find these especially helpful). The mandalas contain universal symbols, which are explained on the pages following each meditation, but you may also discover symbolism that is personal to you. As you meditate, you can use your knowledge of the universal symbols to guide your reflections, but it is more important to work with the mandalas intuitively, simply allowing their meaning to enter your unconscious mind. As you progress, you will find that by visually contemplating the mandalas and not over-analyzing what you see, you will allow them to communicate with you at a deeper, more primal level.

The mandalas are not shown in any particular order. Just choose one that feels right for the moment. Your choice may be based on visual appeal or the symbolism may be more important. On the CD the same mandalas are reproduced in a stunning 3D format, for a really intense meditative experience via a computer screen (see page 13). There is also an (optional) soundtrack for those who find soothing background sounds help them to relax into the meditation.

When people start to meditate they are sometimes disappointed because they feel that they are not making sufficient progress. Remember that even if you have not yet reaped an obvious benefit, you will already be changing at an unconscious level. However, don't worry if you decide that now is not the right time in your life for you to practise meditation. You can always return to it at a later date.

The guidelines on the next page are not hard-and-fast rules but are intended to help you get the most out of your practice.

Tips for meditating

❂ Try not to rush your meditations – they do not need to take a long time, but it is best if you set aside a special time and place where you will be free from interruptions. That way, you can really focus and will be less tempted to think about all the things you have to do.

❂ Find a comfortable posture so that you won't fidget. Try sitting in a chair or cross-legged on the floor, with your back straight and your hands palm upward in your lap.

❂ Place the mandala where you can see the detail clearly.

❂ Look at the mandala with a relaxed gaze, taking in the whole image before focusing on one spot – usually just above the centre.

❂ Resist any thoughts or external stimuli that start to intrude. If distractions arise, just bring your attention back to the mandala.

❂ As you meditate, just notice whatever arises. (However, if you find yourself troubled by especially disturbing thoughts, it may be a good idea to stop this meditation and choose a mandala that is more suited to your state of mind.)

❂ When you feel ready, shift your attention to another detail of the mandala and contemplate this, taking your time.

❂ As you go deeper into the mandala do not strive to achieve insights, but simply let the mandala communicate with you. You are simply *viewing* it, allowing the mandala to communicate at a deep level of the unconscious mind.

❂ If you become very advanced in your meditation practice, you will be able to transcend the physical body into a state of pure consciousness, freed from the constraints of the senses.

❂ When you are ready, slowly bring your attention back to the everyday world. You may like to end your meditation with a short prayer or some other closing ritual.

Using the CD

On the CD accompanying this book you will find:

❋ 3D versions of the 12 mandalas that appear in this book.

❋ 2D versions of the same mandalas, suitable for people who want to meditate looking at enlarged versions of the regular images on screen.

❋ Soothing soundtrack (including chanting and ocean sounds) to enhance your meditation experience.

❋ Meditation timer. Click on 5, 10, 15, 20, 25 or 30 minutes to set the timer to chime after the desired period. Click play to start the timer running, and click pause or stop if you want to interrupt it.

The 3D mandalas have been designed to bring about a new level of awareness in your meditation. Each 3D mandala artwork is composed of a pair of slightly offset images. To experience the artwork in three dimensions, you will need to use the special glasses provided. The red- and blue-coloured filters allow one offset image to enter the left eye and the other to enter the right eye; the brain then combines the two images to give 3D perception – the illusion of depth. Because everyone's brain works differently, some people experience a more pronounced 3D effect than others. If you find the 3D experience uncomfortable or disconcerting, you could use the enlarged 2D artworks instead.

Caution

Set the timer to ensure that you don't meditate using the 3D images and the computer screen for too long. If you know that you suffer from eyestrain or any medical condition (for example, migraine or photosensitive seizures), you are advised to exercise particular caution. The majority of people are unlikely to experience problems when following these instructions, but if you encounter any visual disturbance, headache or other unusual symptoms, end your meditation immediately and seek medical advice if your symptoms continue.

SETTING THE SPIRIT FREE

According to Buddhist thought, animals have the potential
for enlightenment, and the doctrine of rebirth means
that humans can be reborn as animals and vice versa.
This meditation allows you to escape from your earthly
distractions and let your spirit soar.

1

Consider Buddha's Bodhi Tree with its roots anchored deep in the
ground and its vast, leafy branches extending in all directions. Open
your mind to your ability to transcend your origins and the density
of the material world.

2

Look at the birds swooping and diving, and feel their energy as they
rejoice in their freedom, dipping in and out of the sunlight in the clear
blue sky. The birds are within you and you are within the birds.

3

In your mind enter the quiet shade of one of the sacred temples located
in the corners of the mandala and allow yourself to relax there without
distractions from inside yourself or the outside world.

4

Meditate and you will find within yourself the strength of the Bodhi Tree
rising from the soil of incarnation and reaching toward the light.

THE BODHI TREE

In Buddhism, the Bodhi Tree was the tree beneath which Siddhartha Gautama sat in meditation for 49 days around 2,500 years ago. There he faced the demon Mara, who tried to tempt him with seductive illusions, before he attained the state of enlightenment or *Bodh*. From that time on he was known to his followers as the Buddha or "Awakened One". After enlightenment the Buddha continued to sit in meditation beneath the Bodhi Tree for one more week. The original tree at Bodh Gaya in India is said to have been destroyed by King Pusyamitra during his persecution of Buddhism in the 2nd century BCE, but many such trees – their botanical name is *ficus religiosa*, meaning "sacred fig" – have since been planted in the grounds of Buddhist temples as symbols of the Buddha's presence and as objects of worship. Taking between 100 and 3,000 years to reach their full size, sacred figs are recognizable for their heart-shaped leaves and complex branches and roots (the root system below the ground is as wide as the canopy it supports).

"Accept whatever happens and
let your spirit move freely."

CHUANG TZU (C. 369–286 BCE)

"There are only two benefits we
can hope to give to our children.
One is roots; the other, wings."

HODDING CARTER (1907–1972)

BEYOND EARTHLY BEAUTY

Learning to value ourselves and feel love and compassion
for others is the foundation for spiritual progress in the
journey to enlightenment. In this meditation we reach beyond
earthly beauty and impermanence to find all-sustaining,
unconditional love, and peace beyond the physical world.

1

Contemplate the cloudburst of exquisitely formed cherry blossom,
which embodies hope and all that is feminine and exuberant in nature.
Take it into your mind as the flowering of self-awareness and your
many-petalled self. Notice the flowers that lie strewn on the water – the
scattering of physical perfection in the breeze.

2

Turn your awareness to the paving stones and see how their irregular,
solid shapes contrast with the flowers' soft, pink petals. Despite their
unevenness, the stones interlock perfectly – a symbol of
unconditional love and its tolerance of imperfection.

3

In the calm, reflective waters discover who you are, without judgment,
fear or pretence.

4

The bridges lead to a lush, green land where you may embark on the final
stage of your journey – represented here by the pagodas, their pointed
roofs symbolizing the spirit ascending to heavenly bliss.

CHERRY BLOSSOM

The flowers of the cherry tree bloom in abundance, but only for a very short time. In Japan this ephemeral blossom is both celebrated for its delicate beauty and wistfully mourned as a poignant symbol of all that is transient in life – a concept that is closely associated with Buddhist thought. The symbol extends to the Japanese samurai tradition, as these fearless warriors often met an untimely and violent death (the petals are seen as falling like so many drops of blood). The flower has great cultural significance for the Japanese, having attained the status of an unofficial national emblem. Every spring, crowds gather in public parks and gardens to picnic below the cherry blossom in a centuries-old blossom-viewing custom known as *hanami*. By contrast, in China cherry blossom represents spring, hope, youth, virility, feminine beauty and the feminine principle.

"Listen to the voice of nature,
for it holds treasures for us all."

SAYING OF HURON PEOPLE OF NORTH AMERICA

"In the cherry blossom's shade there
is no such thing as a stranger."

KOBAYASHI ISSA (1763–1827)

BIRDS OF FORTUNE

Although our lives are sometimes overshadowed by events
that cloud our happiness, eventually good times return and
our troubles vanish. In contemplating the cranes as a symbol
of good fortune, this meditation focuses on maintaining
hope and on giving thanks for our blessings.

1

Look at the various elements in the mandala: the central figures of
the faithful crane and her lifelong mate with legs and bills entwined;
the outer ring of cranes, present by day and by night; and the clouds
that sometimes partially obscure the birds.

2

Keep the mandala in your field of vision, but let the details fade from
your eyes as the vast blue sky fills your mind.

3

Visualize the clouds floating across your consciousness in random
formation, and then visualize a flock of cranes passing in and out
of the clouds. Each magnificent bird that emerges from the mist is
bringing good fortune and creative solutions to your problems.
You are at peace and give thanks.

CRANES

The crane is a symbol of peace, loyalty, creativity and wisdom. In ancient Greece, this elegant bird was associated with Apollo, patron of music and poetry, as a herald of spring and light. According to another ancient European legend, cranes gather by night in a circle to protect their leader. They stay awake by standing on one leg, holding the other leg raised with a stone clasped in the claw. Should one of the sentinels fall asleep, the stone will fall, waking the sleeper. These beautiful birds perform a spectacular courting dance and mate for life, which in China and Japan is fabled to be a thousand years. It was believed in ancient China that Taoist priests transformed after death into cranes and that the souls of the deceased were carried on the back of a crane to the sky. In Japan the crane is a symbol of good fortune, and a thousand paper cranes are traditionally given as a wedding gift, to wish the newly united pair a thousand years of happiness and prosperity.

"Fortune will call at the smiling gate."

JAPANESE PROVERB

"He who folds a thousand origami
cranes will be granted a wish."

JAPANESE PROVERB

4

TIME AND THE UNIVERSE

In today's hectic world, our minds are so full of the things we need to do that we are often unable to enjoy the present moment. This meditation invites you to slow down and forget the clock, and instead view time as the eternal flow of the universe.

1

Take a few minutes to identify the various elements of the mandala. The flow of water – constant yet endlessly changing – represents time. The seasons with their different colours and rhythms are present in the falling leaves. Notice the spheres spinning among the stars, symbolizing the grand cycles of the galaxy. Finally, find the butterfly (whose life is briefer than ours), the tree (whose life is longer), the spiral (standing for infinite time) and the mathematical symbol for infinity.

2

Holding the mandala in your field of vision, imagine all these different aspects of time, with their separate meanings, dissolving into the swirling river, the cosmic flow.

3

Feel yourself immersed in the river, becoming one with it. The mandala is a single drop of water, a single moment in an infinite number of moments. Relax in this moment and the endlessness of time and space.

TIME AND SPACE

According to Buddhist thought, time as we know it does not exist. Time is inseparable from things and things are constantly changing, so time has no real substance. Humans only give substance to time by labelling it as "past", "present" and "future". Time in Buddhism has no beginning or end; instead it is a succession of infinitesimally small, independent moments that are all relative to each other. While a butterfly may be content to live for only a week, a human may curse the confines of time and feel that a long life is not long enough. But Buddhism sees no difference between life and death, as it holds that throughout our lives we are all living and dying in the same moment and the cycles of life and rebirth are limitless. Just as space cannot be measured, time also is without bounds. By understanding this ultimate truth, we can be liberated from the boundaries of time, defined in seconds, minutes, hours, days, weeks, months and years, and from the confines of space, defined by the directions north, south, east and west.

"Every instant of time is a pinprick of eternity."

MARCUS AURELIUS (121–180 CE)

"The butterfly counts not months
but moments, and has time enough."

RABINDRANATH TAGORE (1861–1941)

5

TO FORGIVE
AND FORGET

Water is the fluid within all living things. It is equated with the continual flux of the manifest world, the unconscious mind, forgetfulness and purification. In this meditation the chalice of plenty at the heart of the mandala pours forgiveness, washing away old grievances so that peace can enter your heart.

1

Begin by contemplating the spiral on the golden chalice of plenty at the centre of the mandala. This is your self, a vortex charged with energy and glowing with warmth and the potential to heal the past.

2

Notice how the chalice of plenty spills its ever-flowing waters, which twist and turn in every direction to bring motion and change, overcoming obstacles and washing away ill-feeling.

3

Meditate on the perfect pattern of reconciliation made by the swirling patterns of forgiveness as they form around your heart in a geometry of love and peace.

4

As you flow out from the circle of potentiality – the table on which the chalice stands – you reach the first circle of the waters, where you find forgiveness in your heart. As you reach the outer circle of the waters, you discover paired doves and the commitment to enact forgiveness.

THE CHALICE

According to Irish legend, the chalice known as the Cauldron of Dagda grants the wishes of all those who come into its presence. In Arthurian legend, the quest for the chalice in the form of the Holy Grail, and the need to prove oneself worthy of it, are a central theme. Christian belief traditionally holds that the Holy Grail is the cup from which Christ drank at the Last Supper; alternatively, it is the receptacle used to collect the blood from Christ's side during the Crucifixion. Through this connection to life-blood, the chalice also has strong associations with the heart. The chalice is sacred, and drinking from it is a means to salvation. It is often seen as an inexhaustible supply of sustenance, containing the draught of life itself. In the sacred art of the Hindu religion, the four sacrificial cups of the Vedas (ancient scriptures) represent the four rivers of paradise.

You can bring the symbolism of the chalice into your own life by considering your soul as a vessel – its precious contents are overflowing with the capacity for doing good and making amends.

"Forgiveness is the giving,
and so the receiving, of life."

GEORGE MACDONALD (1824–1905)

"The weak can never forgive. Forgiveness
is the attribute of the strong."

MAHATMA GANDHI (1869–1948)

6

FOLLOW YOUR DREAMS

The dragon's fire is the primal energy of the physical world. In this meditation, contemplating this powerful, far-sighted and wise creature may help you to move with courage, enthusiasm and decisiveness toward your goals in life.

1

Focus on the centre of the mandala. Feel the warmth and energy of the divine sun that nourishes and drives your earthly being.

2

As you shift your gaze outward to the planets of the solar system, consider the vastness of the cosmos of which we on Earth are just a small part. Your thirst for knowledge and drive to test your own limits are powerful forces, and if you handle them wisely, you can achieve great things.

3

Now moving outward, away from the gravitational pull of the sun, you come to a new plane beyond the darkness of space.

4

Here, in the heavenly realm, meditate on the dragons whose supreme knowledge may bring you closer to your goals and, ultimately, to enlightenment.

THE DRAGON

The dragon is a mythical creature appearing in both Western and Eastern traditions. In European folklore it is usually portrayed as a fire-breathing monster against which heroes must fight – a much feared and destructive force, and the guardian of treasure hoards and portals of esoteric knowledge. In the past, Christianity has played on the dragon's serpent-like qualities by equating it with evil, and representing any subjugation of a dragon as a victory over paganism and heresy. In Celtic mythology, however, the dragon symbolizes sovereignty. Pendragon, meaning "chief dragon", was the name of several kings of the Britons, and the red dragon is the national emblem of Wales. In Eastern thought the dragon is a more benevolent, celestial power. For Taoists and Buddhists the dragon's roar across the heavens dispels delusions, and hence the dragon represents enlightenment and the spiritual essence of the universe. The Chinese dragon is a symbol of luck and good fortune that is paraded through the streets to celebrate New Year; it also represents the dual nature of being – light and dark, creation and destruction, male and female, and the unification of these opposites.

"It is not because things are
difficult that we do not dare;
it is because we do not dare
that they are difficult."

SENECA (C. 4 BCE–65 CE)

"Life can only be understood backward;
but it must be lived forward."

SØREN KIERKEGAARD (1813–1855)

7

LETTING GO
OF FEAR

Worries about our current situation or the future can cloud our
judgment and even paralyze us with fear. In this meditation,
the Buddhist goddess Green Tara, who represents compassion
and enlightened activity, invites you to find a peaceful place
of refuge before embarking on a wise course of action.

1

Look at the goddess and notice her foot poised in readiness to leave the
meditation pose and help the needy. Acknowledge that your feelings
right now are natural, and will not last.

2

Her right hand is turned upward in a gesture of charity and generosity,
while her left hand is in the protective *mudra* (hand gesture), dispelling
fear. As you focus on Tara, allow yourself to be bathed in her wisdom and
loving kindness.

3

Let your troublesome thoughts fade into the background as you
take a moment to still your mind and just be in the present moment,
appreciating the many good things in your life right now.

4

Now focus on the blue lotus that Tara is holding. It symbolizes purity
and the power of perfect wisdom to help you to make your decisions
calmly and with insight.

TARA

It is thought that Tara entered Buddhism from Hinduism in around the 4th century CE. Today, Tara is the generic name in tantric meditation for a set of female *bodhisattvas* (enlightened beings) displaying Buddhist virtues, of which the Green and White Taras are perhaps the best known. According to this tradition Tara was born from the tears of compassion shed by the *bodhisattva* Avalokiteshvara as he looked at those suffering in the world. The story goes that his tears formed a lake in which a lotus grew, and when the flower opened the goddess was revealed. Tara is thus associated by her origins with mercy and compassion. The roles of Green and White Tara are slightly different: the youthful, energetic Green Tara responds to people with worldly concerns by dispelling their fears and anxieties and helping them to overcome dangers, while the motherly White Tara assists those suffering from mental or physical illness.

"In the world deluded by ignorance, the supreme all-knowing one, the Tathagata, the great physician, appears, full of compassion."

LOTUS SUTRA (1ST CENTURY CE)

"... a bodhisattva who is full of pity and concerned with the welfare of all beings, who dwells in friendliness, compassion, sympathetic joy and even-mindedness."

PERFECTION OF WISDOM IN 8,000 LINES (C. 100 BCE–100 CE)

8

TRANSFORMING LOVE

The butterfly is the archetypal image of transformation and can be used to inspire our awakening from the dominance of the ego to a mature self-awareness. It is often associated with love. This meditation will enable you to turn your energies both inward to truth and outward to compassion.

1

Let your eye settle on one of the butterflies at random and in your mind trace its life cycle backward: from adult to chrysalis (pupa), from chrysalis to caterpillar (larva) and from caterpillar back to egg.

2

Focus on the caterpillar at the centre of the mandala – as it devours everything within its reach, it fuels its potential for radical change.

3

As you absorb the image of the mandala into yourself, consider the possibility of change that is inherent in you.

4

Sense your capacity for giving and receiving love in abundance, and visualize yourself bringing joy into your life as well as the lives of other people. Relish these thoughts and the blessings that such love will bring you.

THE BUTTERFLY

The metamorphosis of the butterfly from a tiny egg to a voracious caterpillar, and then from a dormant chrysalis to a winged and gloriously coloured imago (adult), is a universal symbol of transformation from the mundane to the celestial. Although many adult butterflies live for only a week or two, for the Chinese the butterfly is often seen as a symbol of longevity and when portrayed with a chrysanthemum it represents beauty in old age. In both Chinese and Japanese culture, the butterfly has for centuries represented the essence of happiness, especially in love and relationships. Many ancient civilizations, such as the Celts, saw the human soul as a butterfly, and butterflies feature widely in myth and legend, sometimes bringing sleep and dreams, sometimes as a potent fertility symbol. In religious art a butterfly may be shown in the hand of the Christ Child as a symbol of resurrection. According to chaos theory the beating of a butterfly's wings can cause a knock-on effect that alters the course of a hurricane on the other side of the world. Thus, even the smallest change can have far-reaching effects as all things are connected.

"The soul stirs within its chrysalis, dreaming
that it will one day be an angel. It will."

LOU ANDREAS-SALOMÉ (1861–1937)

"One word frees us of all the weight
and pain of life – that word is 'love'."

SOPHOCLES (C. 497–405 BCE)

9

THE LION'S COURAGE

Confronting our fears and resisting our most powerful instincts – to fight or to take flight – can be a source of strength in difficult times. In this meditation you will find the lion's courage in yourself.

1

The lion with its open jaws is fierce and frightening. Recognize something of yourself in this untamed beast – your animal nature, from which your instincts stem.

2

Notice the spiral and light at the very centre of the mandala, which emanate from deep within the lion's mouth, representing nature's energy and the solar power that is so often associated with the lion.

3

Allow your gaze to rest on the lion's teeth. You too have weapons, but remember that you also have love, knowledge and faith to serve you well.

4

Realize that the lion's roar is intended as a deafening show of force, but your silent inner strength is more powerful.

5

Now look at the battlements that encircle the lion's head. These represent the defences that will protect your soul from harm.

THE ELEMENTS

According to Classical thought, the four elements – earth, fire, air and water – are the building-blocks of the universe. To these a fifth element, unchanging ether (representing the spirit or the self) is sometimes added. Throughout history the elements have been considered important in many disciplines, including alchemy, Western astrology, Indian Ayurveda and the Chinese system of geomancy known as feng shui. In the context of human nature, earth represents stability, materialism and realism; in astrology, earth zodiac signs are practical and dependable and have a deep affinity with nature. Fire symbolizes passion, energy, impulse, enthusiasm, inspiration, idealism and faith; fire signs are the motivational movers and shakers of the zodiac, with much creative energy. Air symbolizes mental processes, language, intellect, reason, communication and social relationships; air signs are the thinkers whose ideas can shape world events. Water is associated with psychic powers, mysticism and intuition; water signs are said to be creative and nurturing. Earth and water are associated with the feminine principle, while air and fire have masculine energy.

"To see a world in a grain of sand
And a heaven in a wild flower ..."

WILLIAM BLAKE (1757–1827)

"All things are parts of one single system, which
is called nature; the individual life is good
when it is in harmony with nature."

ZENO (4TH CENTURY BCE)

REGENERATION

The human body has enormous power to heal itself and to regenerate. By finding tranquillity in meditation, you can help the body to deal with illness and repair injury, as well as allowing the mind to manage stress, listlessness and depression. Like the phoenix we can arise anew.

1

The phoenix represents your invincible spirit. Think of its fabulous feathers stroking your body with a magic, healing touch.

2

Allow your gaze to rest on the apple and the fruit of the bountiful earth. Choose wisely and nature can provide nourishment to make you well.

3

Now find the white dove with outstretched wings that signifies your inspiration, faith and hope for the future.

4

Finally, meditate on the triangle of twigs enclosing a dot. This is the emblem of transforming elemental fire, which burns away your fears, bad habits and sickness and enables you to find liberation. Let your worries melt away as you meditate on the invincible core of your true self.

THE PHOENIX

Rising from the ashes to be reborn, the phoenix is a universal symbol of resurrection and immortality. According to Egyptian legend the phoenix might live for five centuries, but only one of these magnificent creatures could exist at any one time. When the end of its life was drawing near, it would build a nest of cinnamon twigs and sing so beautifully that the sun god rising in the east was made to pause in his journey. When a spark from the sun's rays set the nest alight, the phoenix would die, but after three days it would be reborn and offer its ashes in homage to the sun god. As the firebird, the phoenix also symbolizes divine nobility and has been associated with Christ's resurrection from the fires of the Passion, and the awakening of spiritual faith. Like the dragon, the phoenix is made up of elements that typify the cosmos: it has the head of a cock (the sun) and the back of a swallow (linked to the crescent moon); its wings are associated with the wind, its tails with trees and flowers, and its feet with the earth.

"Natural forces within us are
the true healers of disease."

HIPPOCRATES (C. 460–370 BCE)

"Oh joy! that in our embers
Is something that doth live ..."

WILLIAM WORDSWORTH (1770–1850)

LOTUS JOURNEY

In Eastern traditions the lotus is a symbol of the unsullied heart or soul, rising from the muddy waters of human imperfections. Our inner beauty, once we nourish it, blossoms to reveal astonishing purity. This meditation focuses on our journey to spiritual growth.

1

Rest your eyes on the very centre of the lotus. This is the stamen – the life centre by which the flower is pollinated and through which the plant can reproduce. Think about your own inner life force – your ability to be reborn at a spiritual level.

2

Now contemplate the petals themselves. Traditionally, lotus petals are used to symbolize the chakras – in yoga philosophy, these are the energy centres of the subtle (non-physical) body. Think of this mandala's lotus petals as representing your own energetic body. Reflect on each of the seven major chakras situated along your spine: the Root, Sacral, Solar Plexus, Heart, Throat, Brow and Crown Chakras (the latter is positioned just above your head), which are alive with healing and transforming power as you grow in spiritual awareness.

3

Shift your gaze to the lotus buds that represent your potential. Notice the fish weaving their way through the reeds and the frogs sitting on the lily pads. The water of life sustains a myriad of life forms, allowing them to develop, and we all have the capacity for transformation.

THE LOTUS

The lotus is the floral emblem of India – in Hinduism a lotus flower grew from the navel of Vishnu and gave birth to Brahma. The lotus is also sacred to Buddha, who is often depicted seated on a lotus throne. Reaching from the murky depths to hold the pristine flowers above the water's surface, the lotus's long stem symbolizes the cord that attaches man to his origins, while the root signifies indissolubility. The lotus plant embodies the past, the present and the future because it bears buds, flowers and seeds all at the same time. In bud it is the heart of man and all potentiality; in full bloom the flower is the cosmic wheel, and depicts spiritual unfolding as the petals open up in the light of heaven; and the lotus's seed pod represents creation and the renewal of life. The colour of the lotus is also symbolic: the white lotus represents spiritual perfection and mental purity; the pink lotus is the supreme lotus associated with the highest deity and the Buddha; red is the lotus of love and compassion associated with purity of the heart; and the blue lotus symbolizes wisdom and the victory of the spirit over the senses.

"A journey of a thousand miles
begins with a single step."

LAO TZU (6TH CENTURY BCE)

"Concealed in the hearts of all beings is the
Atman, the Spirit, the Self; smaller than the
smallest atom, greater than the vast spaces."

KATHA UPANISHAD (C. 800–200 BCE)

TAKING IT FURTHER

Having explored the mandalas within this book, you may decide to make mandala meditation part of your daily routine.

Within this pack is a set of mandala cards, which you can colour in as part of your practice. The act of mindful colouring – paying attention to your visual response to the mandala and to what your experience is in this moment – can be a great way of releasing yourself from unwanted, troubling and habitual thoughts. When you colour mindfully, use colours intuitively – the aim isn't to create a beautiful image, although the result may be aesthetically pleasing. You may even decide to give the cards away to friends and family, or you may want to return to them later for further meditation practice.

Some people like to create their own mandalas from scratch. The Swiss psychiatrist Carl Jung became extremely interested in mandalas and their symbolism, and found that the mandalas created by his clients were highly indicative of their psychological and spiritual health. If you choose to do this, remember that the mandala should be the product of your unconscious mind. Although a mandala often has symmetry and conveys balance and harmony, as with the colouring don't actively try to create an attractive design. The aim is for the mandala to communicate some insights as you meditate on it.

If you are interested in taking your meditation practice further, consider joining a class run by an experienced teacher, who will be able to guide you on your journey.

INDEX